Improving Reading Comprehension
Grade 3

Table of Contents

Introduction

We have all watched a child struggle while learning to read. Each new word can be a challenge or a frustration. We have joined in the child's struggle, teaching the skills needed to decode unfamiliar words and make sense of the letters. Then we have experienced joy as the child mastered the words and began to read sentences, gaining confidence with each new success.

Learning to read is one of the most important skills your students will ever acquire. By the third grade, most children are becoming independent, confident readers. The emphasis now can be placed on practicing the valuable skills of reading comprehension. Readers need to develop the skill of making sense of new words through context. They need to understand an author's message, whether stated or implied. They need to see how each event in a story affects the rest of the story and its characters. These are all important skills that must be nurtured if a student is to be a successful reader. Reading comprehension is vital for success in school and for success in many other areas of life.

The stories in *Improving Reading Comprehension* have been written to interest and engage the readers. These short stories hold the reader's attention. The brief exercises are effective tools for determining the student's understanding of each story. Given as homework or class work, the two-page assignments can easily be incorporated into existing reading programs.

Organization

The stories in *Improving Reading Comprehension* have been divided into six chapters: Seasons, Animal Tales, Pets, Silly Stories and Fairy Tales, All About Animals, and Mystery and Adventure. The stories are a mix of fantasy, nonfiction, and realistic fiction.

The comprehension exercises include completing sentences, matching words with definitions, labeling, finding words with similar meanings, multiple-choice questions, and crossword puzzles. Many exercises emphasize vocabulary development as well. Each story and exercise are complete on two sides of one tear-out sheet.

The Curriculum Correlation chart on Page 4 allows you to integrate the reading exercises into other curriculum areas.

A Letter to Parents is included on Page 5, and a Letter to Students is on Page 6. Notifying students and parents of a new activity beforehand will help answer students' questions and keep parents informed.

The four assessments can be used individually or in any order.

Use

Improving Reading Comprehension is designed for independent use by students. Copies of the stories and activities can be given to individual students, pairs of students, or small groups for completion. They can also be used as a center activity.

To begin, determine the implementation that fits your students' needs and your classroom structure. The following plan suggests a format for this implementation.

1. **Explain** the purpose of the activities to your class.

2. **Review** the mechanics of how you want students to work with the exercises. You may wish to introduce the subject of each article. You may decide to tap into students' prior knowledge of the subject for discussion. You might plan a group discussion after the reading.

3. **Remind** students that they are reading for understanding. Tell them to read carefully. Remind them to use a dictionary when necessary if context clues are not enough to help them figure out a word.

4. **Determine** how you will monitor the Assessments. Each assessment is designed to be used independently. You may administer the assessments to the whole class, to small groups who have completed a unit, or to individuals as they work through the book. The assessments can be used as pre- and post-evaluations of the students' progress.

Additional Notes

1. **Parent Communication.** Use the Letter to Parents, and encourage the students to share the Letter to Students with their parents. Decide if you want to keep the activity pages and assessments in portfolios for conferencing, or if you want students to take them home as they are completed.

2. **Bulletin Boards.** Since a key to comprehension is discussion, encourage students to illustrate, add to, or do further research on their favorite stories. Display the students' work on a bulletin board.

3. **Have Fun.** Reading should be fun, and the stories in *Improving Reading Comprehension* will capture students' interest and stimulate their imaginations. Fun group discussions, ideas, or games that evolve from the reading will enhance the learning experience.

Improving Reading Comprehension
Grade 3

Curriculum Correlation

Story Title	Social Studies	Language Arts	Science	Math	Physical Education
Strawberry Summer	X	X			
Aunt Kate's Cottage		X			
Emergency!	X	X			X
Winter Words		X	X		
Snow Angel		X			
Four Seasons		X	X		
Leaf Leaping		X	X		X
A Bear Scare		X			
Best Friends		X	X		
Just Plain Newton	X	X			
Trading Places	X	X			
Cheese, Please!		X			
A Bad Snack	X	X	X		
Too Many Rabbits!		X	X	X	
Name Game		X			
Class Pet		X	X	X	
The Rocking Chair		X			
Precious Presents	X	X			
Marie's Hen		X	X		
School Story		X			
Goat Grief!	X	X			
The Candlemaker	X	X	X		
The Sand Castle		X			
Winter Wear		X			
Clowning Around	X	X			
The Changing Man		X			
Less Mess		X			
A Gingerbread House		X			
Lost and Found		X	X		
Dogs Deliver!	X	X			
A New Name	X	X			
Going Batty!		X	X		
Oh, Deer!		X			
Don't Bug Me!		X	X		
Cat Facts		X	X		
A Strange Adventure		X			
The Lighthouse		X	X		
Message in a Bottle	X	X			
Night Fright		X			
Wilbur Fapes		X			
Monster Mystery		X	X		
Soapy Business	X	X			

Dear Parents:

Learning to read is clearly one of the most important things your child will ever do. By the third grade, most children are becoming confident, independent readers. They have developed a good sight vocabulary and have learned ways to decode unfamiliar words.

What is equally important for young readers, however, is reading with understanding. If your child reads a story but is unable to describe the events in his or her own words or answer questions about the story, then the reading loses its meaning. Young readers need practice to strengthen their reading comprehension abilities.

With this goal in mind, our class will be working with a book of stories and activities that will reinforce reading comprehension. The short stories are a mix of fiction and nonfiction. The stories are fun and the one-page exercises are varied. Without feeling the pressure of a long story to remember or many pages of exercises to work, your child will develop a better understanding of the reading and have fun doing it!

Occasionally, your child may bring home an activity. Please consider the following suggestions to help your child work successfully.

• Provide a quiet place to work.
• Help your child to find the meanings of difficult words through the context of the story.
• Discuss the story.
• Go over the directions for the exercises together.
• Check the lesson when it is complete. Note areas of improvement as well as concern.

Thank you for being involved with your child's learning. A strong reading foundation will lead to a lifetime of reading enjoyment and success.

Cordially,

Dear Student:

Do you like to read? Remember your favorite story? You could probably tell a friend what happened in the story. Maybe you talked to someone in your family about it.

It is good to think and talk about what you read. This can help you remember. It can also help you to understand what you read.

We will be working with a book of short stories. After reading each one, think about the story. Then answer some questions. Thinking about these stories will help you practice for reading longer stories. It will help you become a better reader.

The stories are a mix of facts and fun. There are animal adventures and stories about pets. There are silly stories and facts about the seasons. You will read mystery and adventure stories. Read carefully and have fun. There is a story here for everyone!

Sincerely,

Assessment 1

Directions

Read the paragraph. Then choose the best word to complete each sentence. Write the word on the line.

Susan opened the door and a blast of cold air hit her face. She did not mind. She dragged her feet through knee-deep snow to the road and started walking slowly to school. She blew and watched her breath form a cloud in the air. She looked around her and thought the snow sparkled like a million tiny diamonds. The morning was silent, and Susan felt peaceful as she walked down the road. Ahead of her, she saw two boys having a snowball fight. Susan did not want to be hit, so she turned to cut across the field behind the school. Once again she was walking in snow that reached her knees.

1. The morning was _____.

    over   soon   silent

2. Susan thought the snow sparkled like _____.

    diamonds   dials   lights

3. Susan felt _____ as she walked down the road.

    hot   tired   peaceful

4. Susan saw two boys having a _____ fight.

    fist   silly   snowball

5. She cut _____ a field.

    around   through   off

Assessment 2

Directions

Read the paragraph. Choose a word from the paragraph with the same meaning as the underlined words. Write the word on the line.

Marie and her Uncle Bob entered the hen house quietly. They didn't want the hens to get excited. They were already noisy enough! Uncle Bob spread some feed on the floor. This got most of the hens off their nests. Marie looked around the dusty hen house. The sunlight filtering in through the cracks in the house gave the only light. She began to gather the warm eggs from the empty nests. She set each egg carefully in her basket. A few hens were still on their nests. They wanted to hatch their eggs. Marie avoided those eggs. She did not want to be pecked! Uncle Bob shooed the birds away and took the remaining eggs. Then they left the little house. Later, Marie would come back to shoo all the hens out of the house and sweep.

1. Marie helped her uncle <u>collect</u> eggs. _____

2. The sunlight <u>sifting</u> through the cracks gave the only light. _____

3. Marie <u>stayed away from</u> the eggs that were still under hens. _____

_____

4. She did not want to be <u>hit by a beak</u>. _____

5. Uncle Bob took the eggs that were <u>left</u>. _____

Assessment 3

Directions

Read the paragraph. Then answer the questions about the story. Circle the letter in front of the correct answer.

Once upon a time, there was a little girl whose room was always very messy. Nothing her mother did could get the girl to keep her room clean. The reason that the girl did not clean her room was that she just didn't think there was any reason to do it. She didn't mind stepping over piles of clothes and toys to get to her bed. She didn't care if her games were all mixed together. She didn't even care on which end of the bed she put her head at night. So why should she clean her room?

1. What did the mother want the girl to do?
   a. the dishes
   b. clean her room
   c. sweep the floor

2. The girl did not clean her room because _____.
   a. she didn't like stepping over her clothes
   b. she didn't like her mother
   c. she didn't think there was any reason to

3. The girl might clean her room _____.
   a. if she lost one of her favorite things
   b. if her mother asked her to
   c. if her games were mixed together

Assessment 4

Directions

Read the paragraph. Then choose a word from the paragraph that fits each clue. Write the words in the puzzle.

There are hundreds of different kinds of bats. They make up a huge portion of the mammals of the earth. Since bats are active at night, many people have never seen one. However, if you happen to live near a bridge that houses a bat colony, you may have seen a spectacular sight. During the warmer summer months, at dusk each day, the entire colony will take wing at once. They fly in swarms from their upside-down perches in search of insects. In some places, this sight is a regular attraction!

ACROSS:
1. large numbers of things in motion
4. warm-blooded animals with fur
5. part

DOWN:
2. something that draws attention
3. a group of animals living together

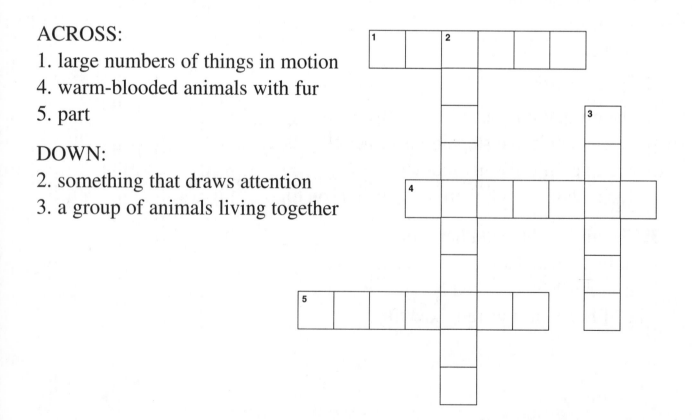

Name _____   Date _____

Strawberry Summer

Last summer I visited my grandparents who live on a farm in Indiana. I had never visited a farm before, and I was looking forward to learning all about it. We drove up a long, winding lane to a tall, old farmhouse. Grandfather and Grandmother came to the car and greeted me with hugs. That evening Grandmother informed me my first project would be picking strawberries. I was so excited I could scarcely sleep.

Early the next morning, Grandfather and I prepared to go to the field. From the barn, we carried heavy boxes in which to pack the strawberries for the market. Then we each chose a large tin pail and walked quietly, with pails swinging, to the edge of an endless green field.

Grandfather said with a smile, "The trick to lasting through the morning is to eat fewer strawberries than you can carry. Now, I will start with this row and you start with the next row. As you pick, gently place your strawberries in the pail to prevent bruising. Remember, Emily, to pick only those berries that are red."

Well, bright red strawberries were everywhere, bursting with color! Many were hiding behind fat, green leaves, where drops of water were sparkling in the early morning sun. I picked my first strawberry and popped it into my mouth. I decided I had  never tasted anything as wonderful as a farm-fresh strawberry.

We both filled our pails five times and carefully packed the strawberries for the market. As we carried the boxes to the farmhouse, I wondered what my next project would be.

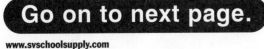
Go on to next page.

Directions

Rewrite each sentence. Use a word with the same meaning from the Word List in place of the underlined words.

Word List

prevent   scarcely   bursting   endless
project   prepared   informed   bruising

1. Grandmother <u>told me</u> what I would be doing. _____

_____

2. My first <u>thing to do</u> would be picking strawberries. _____

_____

3. I was so excited I could <u>barely</u> sleep. _____

_____

4. Grandfather and I <u>got ready</u> to go to the field. _____

_____

5. We walked to the edge of the <u>very long</u> green field. _____

_____

6. The strawberries were <u>very full</u> with color. _____

_____

7. We were gentle with the strawberries to keep them from <u>getting hurt</u>.

_____

8. I could not <u>stop</u> myself from eating the first strawberry I picked! _____

_____

Aunt Kate's Cottage

Lana and her family were packing the car. Today was the first day of summer vacation. Every year, for as long as Lana could remember, her family had gone to the lake for the whole summer. Lana's Aunt Kate owned a cottage there. She always had invited Lana's family to stay with her for the summer.

Lana loved to go to visit her aunt's cottage. It was surrounded by fir trees that were full of birds and their nests. Lana and her brother would spend all day swimming and fishing. At night they would cook dinner over a fire and tell stories by the lake.

As Lana looked out of the car window, she was both happy and sad. She was looking forward to spending the summer at the lake, but this would be their last summer there. Aunt Kate had decided to sell the

cottage. She told the family she would keep it until the end of the summer. Then she was putting the cottage up for sale. Lana would miss the lake and the cottage very much. She promised herself that this summer would be the best summer of all at the lake.

Go on to next page.

Directions ———————————————————————

Answer each question about the story. Circle the letter in front of the correct answer.

1. Where are Lana and her family going?
   a. to the lake
   b. to school
   c. around the country
   d. into the city

2. What do Lana and her brother do all day?
   a. hike
   b. fish and swim
   c. sit under the trees
   d. watch birds

3. Why is Lana sad?
   a. She cannot buy the cottage.
   b. It is not summer vacation.
   c. The lake is far away.
   d. It is to be her last summer at the cottage.

4. What does Lana promise to do this summer?
   a. play in the water each day
   b. make it the best summer of all
   c. help Aunt Kate with the chores
   d. cook dinner every night

5. What might happen so that Lana can visit the cottage next year?
   a. Lana might catch many fish.
   b. Lana's parents might decide to buy the cottage.
   c. Lana might not enjoy the lake.
   d. Lana might meet the new owners.

Emergency!

Kenny looked forward to Thanksgiving Day every year. His grandpa always came to visit. Grandpa would share stories with Kenny, and they would laugh and talk for hours.

One year, after the family had eaten their Thanksgiving meal, Kenny's parents and his brother went to see a movie. Kenny and his grandpa thought about what they could do during the afternoon.

"I know," Kenny said. "Let's play football! I need a lot of practice."

"That sounds like fun," answered Grandpa. "Find the football, and I'll meet you in the yard."

Kenny and Grandpa passed the football back and forth many times. They practiced passing and catching. Suddenly, as Grandpa reached to catch a pass, he fell down.

"Grandpa, what's wrong?" asked Kenny.

"I stepped in a hole and tripped, Kenny," Grandpa answered slowly. "I think I broke my ankle. You will need to call for help."

Kenny hurried into the house to make the call. Beside the telephone he saw a list of telephone numbers. He carefully dialed the number next to the word *emergency*. A man's voice answered at the other end. He asked Kenny several questions and Kenny answered each one.

An ambulance and Kenny's parents arrived at almost the same time. Kenny could see that Grandpa was in good hands.

"We are glad that you were here to help Grandpa," Kenny's parents said. "We are proud of you for taking such good care of him."

Go on to next page.

Directions

Answer each question about the story. Circle the letter in front of the correct answer.

1. Why does Kenny like Thanksgiving Day?
   a. He enjoys all the food.
   b. He likes to watch football.
   c. He spends time with Grandpa.
   d. He reads stories.

2. What do Kenny and his grandpa decide to do?
   a. play football
   b. go to a movie
   c. eat again
   d. talk

3. How does Kenny's grandpa help Kenny?
   a. Grandpa cooks the Thanksgiving meal.
   b. Grandpa feeds Kenny.
   c. Grandpa helps Kenny practice football.
   d. Grandpa throws the football too far.

4. How does Kenny help Grandpa?
   a. He calls for help.
   b. He listens to Grandpa.
   c. He asks the neighbors for help.
   d. He calls his parents.

5. What do you think Kenny told the person on the phone?
   a. that his grandpa is visiting for Thanksgiving
   b. that he likes to play football
   c. that his grandpa needs help, Kenny's name and address
   d. that Thanksgiving Day is his favorite holiday

Winter Words

One snowy afternoon, Andrew and his classmates stood staring out the window, wishing they could go outside. Mr. Kline, their new teacher, watched the students for a few minutes. Suddenly, he thought of an idea.

"What do you see falling from the sky?" Mr. Kline asked.

"Why, it's snow!" answered Andrew. "Haven't you seen snow before?" he asked curiously.

"I have seen snow, but snow is not always the same. I think we need different words to describe the different forms of snow that fall from the sky," replied Mr. Kline.

"I read that the Eskimos have many different words for snow," Andrew added. "How should we decide what to call our different forms?" he wondered.

"We can start by thinking about the beginning of the winter season. When winter begins, and it is not really cold, snow mixed with rain falls. We call it *sleet*. As the weather becomes colder, sleet freezes on the street. We could call it *slice*," suggested Mr. Kline.

"Let me try!" Andrew said eagerly. "When snow is soft and dry, it feels like powder on your nose. We could call it *snowder*!"

"That's great!" replied Mr. Kline. "Are there any more suggestions?" he asked. The students spent the rest of the afternoon making up new words for snow.

Go on to next page.

Directions

Choose the word that best fits each sentence. Write the word in the blank.

1. Andrew and his _____ looked out the window.
   friends   classmates   teacher

2. "Haven't you seen snow before?" he asked _____ .
   cautiously   foolishly   curiously

3. They thought about the beginning of the winter _____ .
   season   seaside   reason

4. The class thought of words to _____ snow.
   stop   describe   decide

5. Mr. Kline says snow falls in different _____ .
   directions   days   forms

6. Snow mixed with rain is called _____ .
   sleet   steep   ice

7. Andrew _____ told the teacher his idea.
   angrily   eagerly   finally

8. Mr. Kline asked for more _____ .
   sugar   suggestions   students

Snow Angel

Susan tied a wool scarf around her neck and put on her mittens. She opened the door and a blast of cold air hit her face. Susan did not mind. She dragged her feet through knee-deep snow to the road and started walking slowly to school.

Susan blew and watched her breath form a cloud in the air. She looked around her and thought the snow sparkled like a million tiny diamonds. The morning was silent, and Susan felt peaceful as she walked down the road. Ahead of her, Susan saw two boys having a snowball fight. She did not want to be hit, so she turned to cut across the field behind the school. Once again she was walking in snow that reached her knees.

Suddenly, she fell face forward into the snow. Susan pushed herself up and looked down at the mark she had left in the snow. This gave her an idea. She turned around and fell backward in a clean, untouched area of snow. Then she opened and closed her arms and legs a few times. Carefully, Susan stood up without ruining her design. She had made an angel in the snow. Susan reached down and wrote: *Susan was here*. Then she brushed the snow off her coat and walked into the school.

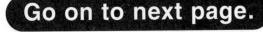
Go on to next page.

Directions

Answer each question about the story. Circle the letter in front of the correct answer.

1. How do you know there is a lot of snow on the ground?
   a. Susan wears a scarf and mittens to school.
   b. The snow sparkles like tiny diamonds.
   c. Cold air hits Susan's face.
   d. Susan walks through knee-deep snow.

2. What does the snow look like to Susan?
   a. a million tiny diamonds
   b. fluffy white clouds
   c. powder
   d. a cloud of cold air

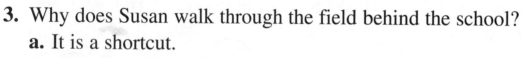

3. Why does Susan walk through the field behind the school?
   a. It is a shortcut.
   b. Boys are throwing snowballs in the road.
   c. She wants to make an angel in the snow.
   d. She wants to write a note in the snow.

4. What does Susan make in the snow?
   a. a snowball fight
   b. tiny diamonds
   c. an angel
   d. a snowman

5. How does Susan feel about the snow?
   a. She enjoys the snow.
   b. She does not like the snow.
   c. She does not notice the snow.
   d. She thinks snow is messy.

Four Seasons

Everyone knows there are four seasons. They are winter, spring, summer, and fall. But the seasons mean different things to people in different parts of the world.

In the northeast of the United States, the seasons change greatly. Summer is a time for going to the beach. The temperature is usually between 70 and 90 degrees. In the fall, the nights cool down quickly. Leaves turn brilliant colors and fall from the trees. Students go back to school. The winter brings freezing rain and snow. The temperatures can fall below zero. Driving can be very dangerous and sometimes impossible. There are many fun outdoor sports to do. It is also very nice to stay inside near a roaring fire! Spring comes slowly. The days get longer and warmer. Spring flowers grow. The birds return from the south.

Near the equator, the seasons barely change at all. Winter, spring, summer, and fall are all hot and often humid. People's habits do not change from one season to the next.

The motion of the earth around the sun causes the seasons. The earth spins as it moves in its orbit. It is also tilted. The northern half of the earth tilts toward the sun in summer. It tilts away from the sun in winter. That  causes the extreme changes in the seasons. It also changes the lengths of the days. They are shorter in winter and longer in summer. The equator is always close to the sun. The days are always about 12 hours long.

The lengths of the days and the temperature of the air during the seasons affect animals and people. For example, birds know that it is time to lay their eggs in the spring. This is because of the longer days. Think about the ways in which the seasons affect you.

Go on to next page.

Directions

Read each clue. Choose a word from the Word List that fits each clue. Write the words in the puzzle.

Word List

seasons   temperature   brilliant   equator
humid   habits   extreme   lengths

ACROSS:

4. degrees of warm or cold
6. four parts of each year, often marked by weather changes
7. very bright
8. things people do regularly

DOWN:

1. very much one way or another
2. hot and moist
3. the imaginary line around the middle of Earth
5. measurements of "how long"

Leaf Leaping

The children looked out the window at the brightly-colored leaves twirling and drifting to the ground. Soon, the ground was lost under a sea of yellow, red, and orange leaves.

Jenny, Paul, and Mike rushed outside and raked the leaves into one large pile. Wanting to get a good run, Jenny started from the corner of the house and ran past the maple tree toward the pile. Just before jumping she took a deep breath and then landed in the leaves. Laughing, she stood up with leaves stuck to her sweater and hair. All three of them raked the leaves back into a pile for the next runner. Mike and Paul each took turns jumping in the leaves.

Suddenly, Jenny ran up and threw a handful of leaves at Mike. Mike grabbed a handful to throw back at Jenny. Soon Paul was throwing leaves, and a leaf war had begun. Before long, the pile of leaves was once again spread all over the lawn. Instead of raking the leaves again, they decided to go inside and rest.

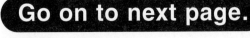

Go on to next page.

Directions

Answer each question about the story. Circle the letter in front of the correct answer.

1. What does the phrase "the ground was lost under a sea" mean?
   a. The ground sinks into the ocean.
   b. Leaves hide the ground.
   c. Leaves look like waves.
   d. It is covered with water.

2. Jenny starts her run from the corner of the house because _____.
   a. she wants to get away from Mike
   b. she needs to hold her breath
   c. the leaves are falling from the tree
   d. she wants to get a good run

3. How do the leaves get all over the lawn again?
   a. The children jump in the leaves.
   b. They fall from the trees.
   c. The children throw them at each other.
   d. The wind carries them.

4. When the children finish playing leaf war, they _____.
   a. go inside
   b. rake up the leaves again
   c. jump into the leaves
   d. watch the leaves fall

5. What time of the year is it in the story?
   a. winter
   b. spring
   c. summer
   d. fall

A Bear Scare

Beaver talked his friend Skunk into going camping in the woods. Beaver had camped many times, but this would be Skunk's first camping trip. Beaver was an expert camper and told Skunk that he would set up their campsite.

Skunk tried to help, but he could not find anything that he could do right. Beaver cut down trees for shelter and for firewood. Then Skunk knocked over the stack of firewood. They went to catch fish for dinner, and Beaver caught a fish. Skunk only caught an old tin can. Skunk decided he was a terrible camper and wanted to stay for only one night.

During the night, Beaver and Skunk woke up when they heard a loud noise. A fierce growl came from the bushes near the shelter. Beaver was terribly frightened. Skunk told Beaver not to worry and crawled out of the shelter. Skunk carefully walked toward the noise.

"Who is there?" asked Skunk.

"GROWL!" something answered.

Skunk quickly turned and sprayed the bushes with his horrible-smelling spray. Suddenly their friend Bear came out of the bushes coughing. Beaver and Skunk scolded Bear for scaring them. Beaver invited Skunk to go camping with him on every camping trip.

Skunk was pleased. "I might be a good camper after all," Skunk thought to himself as he fell asleep.

Go on to next page.

Name _____   Date _____

————————————————————

Answer each question about the story. Circle the letter in front of the correct answer.

1. Who goes on his first camping trip?
   a. Beaver
   b. Skunk
   c. Bear
   d. Skunk's friend

2. Why does Skunk dislike camping?
   a. He cannot do anything right.
   b. Beaver does everything.
   c. It is scary.
   d. Skunk becomes homesick.

3. Who makes the noise that wakes Skunk and Beaver?
   a. Skunk
   b. Beaver
   c. the wind
   d. Bear

4. What does Beaver think about Skunk?
   a. Skunk is very brave.
   b. Skunk is a bad camper.
   c. Skunk is not brave.
   d. Skunk knows how to fish.

5. What is something else that Skunk might be good at doing on a camping trip?
   a. mountain climbing
   b. collecting berries
   c. sledding
   d. building a cabin

Best Friends

Sarah Spider and Beth Bee were best friends. They lived in the same garden and had been friends since they were babies. Sarah was a very talented spider. Her mother had taught her how to spin the most beautiful webs. When she was spinning webs, she was as graceful as a ballerina. Friends often came to watch her spin because she made it look so simple. Artists often came to see the patterns she made in her webs. Sarah was unaware of all the attention. She just loved to spin webs. Her friend Beth was very proud of Sarah's skill. Sometimes, however, Beth felt sad because she did not think she could do anything as well as Sarah.

One day Beth decided to help Sarah spin a web. Beth touched a thread and she became trapped. When she tried to pull free, she tangled a thread around her wings. She ruined the web, and she felt terrible.

Sarah carefully set Beth free. Then they went to their favorite tomato plant to talk.

"How did you get trapped in my web?" Sarah asked. "You frightened me because you could have hurt yourself."

"I am so sorry," Beth cried. "I wanted to spin a web like you do. You spin webs so well, and I don't do anything well."

"There are many things that you could do," Sarah replied. "We will write a list. Then you can choose one thing, and we will find out how to do it!"

The two friends talked all afternoon. They wrote a long list. Then Beth chose one new thing to learn how to do.

Go on to next page.

Directions

Read each sentence. Choose a word from the Word List that has the same meaning as the word or words in bold print. Write the word on the line.

Word List

patterns   graceful   ballerina   simple
unaware   talented   Artists   tangled

1. Sarah was a very **gifted** spider. _____

2. She moved in a **smooth and flowing** way. _____

3. Beth thought she looked like a **dancer**. _____

4. **Creative people** came to see Sarah's webs. _____

5. They liked the **repeating designs** that she made. _____

6. Sarah was **not aware** of all the attention. _____

7. She made it look so **easy**. _____

8. Beth tried to help, but she was **mixed up** in the web. _____

Name_____   Date_____

Just Plain Newton

Newton was a pig. He lived in a pigpen on a farm with many other pigs. Newton looked like the other pigs he knew. This made Newton feel plain and ordinary. Newton wanted to be special. He decided he needed to act differently from the other pigs to be special. So, when the rest of the pigs ate out of the trough, Newton put his food on a plate. When the other pigs relaxed in the mud, Newton would not get himself dirty.

The other pigs did notice Newton, but not in the way that he wanted. Instead of thinking Newton was special, the other pigs made fun of him. They also stopped playing with him.

One day Newton realized acting differently did not make him special. His friends had liked him before he started acting differently. So, Newton went back to his old ways, and soon all the pigs were playing with him again.

Go on to next page.

Directions

Answer each question about the story. Circle the letter in front of the correct answer.

1. Why does Newton feel plain and ordinary?
   a. He does not like the way he looks.
   b. The other pigs tell him he is plain.
   c. He looks like the other pigs.
   d. He cannot do anything special.

2. To be special Newton decides to _____.
   a. act differently
   b. look differently
   c. run away
   d. ignore his friends

3. When the other pigs eat from the trough, Newton _____.
   a. eats from the trough, too
   b. refuses to eat
   c. is first in line
   d. eats off a plate

4. To be special Newton needs to _____.
   a. practice his manners
   b. be himself
   c. change his habits
   d. learn new skills

5. What does Newton learn about himself?
   a. He is just like the other pigs.
   b. He likes to eat off a plate.
   c. He does not like mud.
   d. He is special without acting differently.

Trading Places

A little bird sat on the windowsill. He looked longingly into the house at a bird in its cage. The cage seemed to be such a pleasant place. It had a swing for exercise, a round reflecting mirror, and a little bell that made a sweet sound. There was always water in one dish and food and treats in another. The little bird thought it looked like a wonderful place to live.

Meanwhile, the bird in its cage looked at the world outside his window. He wondered what it would be like to fly free in the sky and land wherever he wanted. He wished he could see what lay beyond his neat backyard and the fence that surrounded it. His people were kind, but he couldn't help feeling the urge to fly out the window and be free.

One day, the people left both the window and the cage door open. The caged bird decided this was his chance. He quickly flew out the window and into the world beyond. At the same time, the free bird flew from the windowsill into the cage. At first, both birds were thrilled. But soon the house bird missed his cage. It was frightening outside! He wasn't sure where to look for food. Besides, the worms and bugs that the other birds were eating almost ruined his appetite! The outside bird felt trapped in the cage. His heart began to beat wildly. All he could think about was getting back outside!

At the first opportunity, both birds returned to their old ways. Now the caged bird looked at the world with new eyes. It was beautiful, but he was happy to look from his perch in the cage. As for the outside bird, he no longer wished to be in the cage. He could hardly believe that he had almost given up his precious freedom for that little space!

Go on to next page.

Directions ————————————————————————

Rewrite each sentence. Use a word with the same meaning from the Word List in place of the underlined words.

Word List
freedom   opportunity   reflecting   longingly
pleasant   precious   appetite   urge

1. The bird on the windowsill looked <u>with longing</u> at the cage in the house.

   _____

2. The cage looked like a <u>nice</u> place to live. _____

   _____

3. The cage had a <u>showing back a picture</u> mirror. _____

   _____

4. The caged bird had the <u>wanting</u> to go outside. _____

   _____

5. The birds traded places at the first <u>chance</u>. _____

   _____

6. The house bird's <u>hunger</u> was ruined when he saw what the other birds ate.

   _____

7. The caged bird knew that his home was <u>dear</u> to him. _____

   _____

8. The outside bird loved his <u>choice to go wherever he wanted</u>. _____

   _____

Cheese, Please!

Milly the mouse poked her head out of her mouse hole. She carefully looked all around the kitchen, watching for Jep the cat. Jep was nowhere to be seen.

"Good!" Milly thought. "Now is a good time to eat the Swiss cheese on the kitchen table."

Milly scurried across the kitchen floor. Just as she reached the leg of the table, Jep crawled out from behind the washing machine where he had been hiding. Jep slowly moved closer to Milly. Milly looked all around the kitchen for a way to escape. From where she was, there was no way to reach her mouse hole. Not knowing what else to do, Milly scampered up the table leg just as Jep pounced. She dove into one of the holes in the cheese as Jep landed on the table. He looked all over the table and the kitchen, but he could not find her. Jep knew she had not made it back to her mouse hole, so he decided to go back to his bed and wait for her. As Jep sat waiting for Milly to come out of hiding, he became tired and soon fell fast asleep.

Meanwhile, Milly was still in the Swiss cheese, greedily nibbling all she could eat. When she had eaten her fill, she poked her head out of the cheese and looked for Jep. She saw him sleeping soundly in his bed. Milly crawled back down to her mouse hole, a very happy mouse.

Go on to next page.

Directions

Answer each question about the story. Circle the letter in front of the correct answer.

1. Why does Milly look around the kitchen?
   a. She wants to know where the cheese is.
   b. The kitchen looks different.
   c. Milly is watching for Jep the cat.
   d. Milly is looking for a friend.

2. What does Milly want from the table?
   a. a drink of water
   b. Swiss cheese
   c. Jep
   d. a hiding place

3. Where is Jep hiding?
   a. behind the washing machine
   b. under the table
   c. on top of the table
   d. next to the mouse hole

4. Why does Milly hide in the cheese?
   a. She wants to eat it.
   b. There is no other place to hide.
   c. Milly wants to surprise someone.
   d. A noise frightens her.

5. Milly knows it is safe to go back to her mouse hole because _____.
   a. she is finished eating cheese
   b. Jep is gone
   c. she hears her friends
   d. Jep is asleep

A Bad Snack

"I don't know why we have to go see the old mice anyway," complained Benny Mouse, scowling. "It's boring!"

"I like it," his sister Shelly said as she walked through the field. "Mabel and Marvin know so much! You never know when they'll tell you something really interesting."

"I suppose that's why you know so much," Benny grumbled. "I'm hungry. Did you bring any food?"

"Mom said wait until dinner. Maybe if you spent less time moaning about and finding fault, you'd enjoy things more," said Shelly. They were almost at Mabel and Marvin's house now.

Just then, Shelly saw Benny preparing to take a bite out of a big red mushroom. "Benny!" she cried. "Don't eat that mushroom! That's poisonous!"

"It is?" said Benny in surprise, skittering away from the mushroom. "How do you know? Maybe you're just trying to keep me starved. Are you absolutely sure?"

"Yes, I am. I learned it from Mabel the last time we came here. She taught me everything about the different kinds of mushrooms, and that one is bad!"

"Humph!" said Benny. She was right again! And old Mabel told her! Well, maybe Marvin could teach Benny a thing or two, he thought. Benny decided to start listening more. Soon he might be a know-it-all like his sister!

Go on to next page.

Name _____   Date _____

Directions ━━━━━━━━━━━━━━━━━━━━━━━━━━━━━━━

Choose the word that best fits each sentence. Write the word in the blank.

1. Benny was angry and _____.
   sour   scowling   scratching

2. He _____ when he talked.
   gagged   laughed   grumbled

3. He thought it was _____ to visit the old mice.
   boring   bowling   fun

4. Shelly said that Benny should not find _____ with everything.
   fresh   food   fault

5. Benny said he was so hungry he was _____.
   sick   stopping   starved

6. He almost bit into a _____ mushroom.
   pink   rotten   poisonous

7. Shelly's cry sent him _____ away from the mushroom.
   sliding   falling   skittering

8. Shelly was _____ sure that the mushroom was bad.
   absolutely   always   not

Too Many Rabbits!

Wendy had rabbits in a hutch behind her house. She had named them Lester, Louie, and Larry. She loved to visit the rabbits, and she took good care of them. One morning Wendy went out to feed her rabbits. She could not find Louie. She looked carefully into a dark corner of the shelter. She saw something very surprising! Louie had babies! Wendy was excited about the babies. She had thought that her rabbits were all male rabbits. She decided to change Louie's name to Louise.

Wendy kept a careful eye on Louise and her babies. Her father helped her build a new hutch. Now a wire wall separated Louise from Lester and Larry. Wendy wanted to protect the five babies. A few days later, Wendy had a new surprise. Lester had babies, too! Now Wendy knew she had two female rabbits and one male! She changed Lester's name to Leslie. She put her in with Louise. Suddenly she had three grown rabbits and nine babies. Her parents said it was too many rabbits!

Wendy put up a sign at school to advertise the rabbits. *Free Rabbits*, it said. Very quickly, she had four students interested in her rabbits. Jeannie wanted one. Rob and Tyra each wanted two. Junie wanted three. Wendy's parents said she could keep one. Wendy's rabbit troubles were solved!

Go on to next page.

Directions

Read each clue. Choose a word from the Word List that fits each clue. Write the words in the puzzle.

Word List

shelter   female   protect   separated

hutch   solved   male   advertise

ACROSS:

3. mother rabbit

7. kept apart

8. keep safe

DOWN

1. father rabbit

2. found the answer

4. to tell people about something; usually to sell something

5. a safe place out of the weather

6. a rabbit house

Name Game

The Syms children had always wanted a dog. They asked their parents several times, and their parents told the children that a dog would need good care. The children promised their parents that they would take good care of a dog by themselves. Since there were five of them, the children were sure that this would not be a problem. Finally, the parents took the family to the animal shelter, and they chose a furry, white dog.

Now the children had to choose a name that everyone liked. Tim, the oldest, thought *Neptune* was a good name. Irene suggested the name *Sport*. Grace wanted to call the dog *Button*. Edward thought that *Button* was silly; he liked the name *Scout*. Rachel, the youngest, wanted to name the dog *Spice*.

Then Tim came up with an idea. "Let's use the first letter of each of our own names to name the dog," he said.

"I will agree if we start with the youngest and end with the oldest," said Rachel.

"*R-E-G-I-T*," said Irene. "That's not a name!"

"No, it isn't, but the letters *T-I-G-E-R* spell a name," said Grace.

The children agreed that *Tiger* would be a good name for the dog.

Go on to next page.

Directions

Answer each question about the story. Circle the letter in front of the correct answer.

1. What do the parents say about having a dog?
   a. They cannot find one they like.
   b. A dog needs good care.
   c. They do not know where to find a dog.
   d. They do not know where to keep the dog.

2. What problem do the children have, once they find a dog?
   a. how to take the dog home
   b. how to choose a name for the dog
   c. deciding whom the dog belongs to
   d. learning what kind of dog they have chosen

3. Tim comes up with the idea of _____.
   a. pulling names out of a hat
   b. letting the youngest family member name the dog
   c. using letters from all of their names
   d. not naming the dog

4. The children finally decide on the name _____.
   a. Whitey
   b. Sport
   c. Regit
   d. Tiger

5. Why is agreeing on a name important to the children?
   a. The dog is everyone's pet.
   b. They promised their parents they would take care of the dog.
   c. They have never named a dog before.
   d. They didn't like the name the dog had before they got it.

Class Pet

Mr. Romero's class decided that they needed a pet for their room. Mr. Romero said that a pet would be fine if the students were prepared to take care of it. They would also have to raise the necessary money.

The first thing the class did was decide what kind of pet they would like. Lyda suggested a gerbil or a hamster. Jeremy thought fish would be good pets. Michael wanted the class to get a turtle. The children discussed many ideas. Finally, they decided to get a lizard. The kind of lizard they wanted would be expensive, but they thought they could raise the money.

The class had a bake sale. They put up signs. They brought in brownies, cookies, and cupcakes. Their sale was a success. Maria volunteered to buy the lizard over the weekend. Everyone looked forward to Monday. But when Monday came, Maria did not bring in a lizard! The lizard was even more expensive than they had thought. So Maria brought in two hermit crabs. The children were not upset. They had agreed on hermit crabs as a second choice.

The class named the crabs Hermie and Nomad. They put them in their new aquarium. There was sand on the bottom. There were rocks and extra shells. Hermie and Nomad also liked to roam about the classroom. The class learned a lot about hermit crabs. They wanted to care for them properly. The children took turns feeding and caring for the crabs. Hermie and Nomad were often hiding. It was a big event when they peeked out of their shells! Hermie and Nomad quickly became two important members of the classroom!

Go on to next page.

Name_____   Date_____

Directions

Choose a word from the Word List that has the same meaning as the underlined word. Write your choice on the line.

Word List

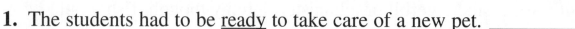

aquarium   discussed   necessary   event
prepared   success   expensive   volunteered

1. The students had to be <u>ready</u> to take care of a new pet. _____

_____

2. They would also have to raise the <u>needed</u> money._____

_____

3. They <u>talked about</u> what kind of pet they wanted. _____

_____

4. The lizard they wanted was <u>worth a lot of money</u>. _____

_____

5. The bake sale was a <u>thing that worked as planned</u>. _____

_____

6. Maria <u>offered</u> to buy the lizard. _____

_____

7. The hermit crabs lived in their <u>glass box</u>. _____

_____

8. It was a big <u>happening</u> when the crabs peeked out of their shells! _____

_____

The Rocking Chair

One day when Beth walked by the nursery, she saw something very strange. The rocking chair was rocking and no one was in the room! Beth thought that the wind must have made the chair rock, but the window was not open.

"Well," said Beth to herself, "there has to be some good explanation!"

The next day, though, the same thing happened. Beth began to think her house was haunted! She told her mother about it, but her mother just laughed.

"I'm sure there is a good reason why that chair was moving, Beth," she said. "Don't be concerned about it."

But Beth was worried—and spooked! How could she sleep near a haunted room? How could her mother put the baby in a haunted room?

Beth decided to hide and spy on the chair. She would catch the ghost in action! Beth hid behind the door and peered out the crack at the room. She was very nervous, but nothing happened for a long time. Then her cat came in the room. The cat was not allowed in the nursery, but Beth kept quiet. She did not want to give herself away. The cat got into the rocking chair. That annoying cat was going to ruin her investigation! She considered shooing away the naughty cat, but just then, her mother approached the doorway. The cat leapt from the chair and under the bed. The rocker rocked! It looked just as it had when Beth saw it. Beth laughed aloud. Now she knew what was haunting the nursery!

Go on to next page.

Name _____   Date _____

Directions

Rewrite each sentence. Use a word with the same meaning from the Word List in place of the underlined words.

Word List

haunted   annoying   nervous   explanation
concerned   ruin   nursery   investigation

1. Beth saw something strange in the <u>baby's room</u>. _____

_____

2. She thought the baby's room might be <u>visited by a ghost</u>! _____

_____

3. Beth's mother told her not to be <u>worried</u>. _____

_____

4. Beth wanted to find a good <u>reason</u> for the moving chair. _____

_____

5. Beth was <u>not comfortable</u> as she hid behind the door. _____

_____

6. Beth's cat was <u>bothering</u> her. _____

_____

7. The cat was going to <u>wreck</u> Beth's plans. _____

_____

8. When the cat jumped, Beth's <u>plan to find out what was going on</u> was complete! _____

_____

Precious Presents

Kathy and her little brother, Robert, waited for their grandmother to come home. She had visited a place called Martha's Vineyard for the summer, and they had missed her very much. Grandma arrived with a big blanket in her arms. "I brought you a present."

"Gammaa, Gammaa!" Robert, who was only two, called as he jumped up and down. Kathy and Robert were very excited.

"What is it, Gram?" Kathy wanted to know. Grandma lifted two small bundles of fur from the blanket. Kathy and Robert gasped. They could not believe what they saw. There were two small kittens.

"Kittens!" Kathy exclaimed.

When the children calmed down, Grandma told them a story. "When I was in Martha's Vineyard, a woman was giving away some kittens. I told her I would like to take two home to my grandchildren." She continued with the story. "These kittens are males, so I have named them Marty and Vinnie, after Martha's Vineyard."

Kathy thought about what Grandma had said. "What a good idea, Grandma."

"Be gentle with the kittens, Robert," Grandma said. She patted the light-colored one. "This one is Vinnie," she told him, and then she stroked the furrier one. "And this one is Marty."

Robert picked one up and held it close. "Marty!" he cried with delight.

Kathy picked up Vinnie. "Thank you, Gram," she said. "We love the kittens from Martha's Vineyard."

Go on to next page.

Directions

Answer each question about the story. Circle the letter in front of the correct answer.

1. Where does Grandma visit for the summer?
   a. Kathy's house
   b. Robert's house
   c. Martha's Vineyard
   d. Grandma's house

2. What does Grandma bring home for the children?
   a. one kitten
   b. two kittens
   c. a blanket
   d. Marty

3. How does the kitten Marty get its name?
   a. from the name Kathy
   b. from the name Grandma
   c. from the name Vinnie
   d. from the name Martha

4. Why does Grandma bring the kittens to Kathy and Robert?
   a. She does not like kittens.
   b. She loves kittens.
   c. Robert likes to pull their tails.
   d. Kathy thinks it's a good idea.

5. Why does Grandma tell Robert to be gentle with the kittens?
   a. They are too big.
   b. He does not like them.
   c. He does not know how to handle them.
   d. He likes Grandma.

Marie's Hen

Marie and her Uncle Bob entered the hen house quietly. They didn't want the hens to get excited. They were already noisy enough! Uncle Bob spread some feed on the floor. This got most of the hens off their nests. Marie looked around the dusty hen house. The sunlight filtering in through the cracks in the house gave the only light. She began to gather the warm eggs from the empty nests. She set each egg carefully in her basket. A few hens were still on their nests. They wanted to hatch their eggs. Marie stayed away from those eggs. She didn't want to be pecked! Uncle Bob shooed the birds away and took the remaining eggs. Then they left the little house. Later, Marie would come back to shoo all the hens out of the house and sweep.

Marie liked gathering the eggs with her uncle. There was something comforting about the warm eggs. She liked the way her basket looked when it was full of the fresh, brown ovals. What she liked the most, though, was the way one of the hens always tagged along behind her. It made her laugh. The little hen would always try to come back in the house while Marie was sweeping it out. It tried to follow her into her uncle's house when she was done. Whenever Marie walked around in the yard, the little hen would appear. If she knelt down in the yard, the little hen would peck at her pockets, looking for corn.

It was clear that the little hen favored Marie. Now Marie couldn't help giving it special treatment. She named the little hen Freckles for the brown spots on its beak. Freckles wouldn't ever play fetch or curl up next to Marie in her bed, but she was Marie's pet just the same!

Go on to next page.

Directions

Choose the word that best fits each sentence. Write the word in the blank.

1. Marie helped her uncle _____ eggs.

    cook   gather   grow

2. The only light in the hen house was from the sun _____ through the cracks.

    filtering   filling   rising

3. Marie thought there was something _____ about the warm eggs.

    strange   confusing   comforting

4. Uncle Bob collected the _____ eggs.

    broken   remaining   regular

5. Marie liked the way the brown _____ looked in her basket.

    oranges   circles   ovals

6. One of the little hens _____ Marie.

    favored   faked   pecked

7. Marie gave the little hen special _____.

    tricks   treatment   clothes

8. Marie's new pet would never play _____.

    fetch   fair   friends

School Story

Jasmine had to write a story for class. She had been home for an hour now and she couldn't think of a thing to write about. How would she get her story done by the next day? While she was thinking, her neighbor came to the door. She wanted to see Jasmine's mom. She brought her dog, Maya. Maya liked to visit with Jasmine's dog, Sadie.

"Jasmine, would you please stay outside with the dogs and make sure they don't run off?" asked Jasmine's mother.

"Mom," Jasmine complained, "I have to do my homework. My story is due tomorrow!" But she went out the door anyway. She could think outside as well as inside, she supposed.

Jasmine watched the dogs. They were amusing to see together. They really were good friends. You could tell they were happy to see each other. They jumped all over each other and fought for the same sticks. They would run around in circles and growl, pretending to be fierce, when really they were just playing. Occasionally, they would hear some noise they thought was unusual and run off to investigate. Jasmine would have to call them back. She gave them each a couple of the bones that were always in her jacket pockets. At first, they each wanted the other dog's bones, but Jasmine got them sorted out and they were happy.

"Just like kids!" Jasmine thought. Then suddenly she had an idea. She would write her story about two good friends—dog friends, that is!

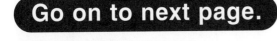

Name_____   Date_____

Directions

Choose a word from the Word List to match each meaning. Write the word on the line.

Word List

occasionally   sorted   amusing   fierce
complained   unusual   due   investigate

1. different _____

2. look into_____

3. funny _____

4. spoke with unhappiness_____

5. wild and dangerous _____

6. supposed to happen _____

7. once in a while_____

8. straightened _____

Goat Grief!

Tim lived on a farm. He did chores before and after school. He didn't mind doing the work, but sometimes he wished he could be more like some of the other boys he knew. Jake didn't have to do much but clean his room occasionally, Chuck's parents seemed to let him do anything he wanted, and Paul's mother was always taking him places. It seemed as if Tim's parents were always either working or too tired to move!

Tim also wished that he could have a pet of his own. There were plenty of animals on the farm, but none of them was actually Tim's. The two dogs were older than he was. Cows weren't good pets, and the goats drove Tim crazy—especially one of the little ones. It chased Tim around the goat pen and jumped up on him. It had quite an appetite, too. Just last week, it stole his favorite cap out of his pocket and chewed a big hole in it before Tim even noticed it was missing. He couldn't stand those goats!

One day, Chuck came home from school with Tim, and he showed Chuck around. At the goat pen, the little goat was up to his usual mischief. It butted Tim with its little head.

Chuck laughed. "It must be fun living on a farm. This place is so great! Look at all these animals. I would love to have a goat for a pet! What a riot!" he said.

Chuck would like a *goat* for a pet? Tim was surprised. He had never thought of the goat as a pet! But he was kind of funny and cute, and he did seem to like to be around Tim! He had never considered that his friends might envy his life the way he sometimes envied theirs. It made him begin to appreciate his life on the farm!

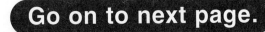
Go on to next page.

Name_____   Date_____

Directions

Read each clue. Choose a word from the Word List that fits each clue. Write the words in the puzzle.

Word List
butted   mischief   envy   appetite
stole   appreciate   grief   considered

ACROSS:

5. took without asking
6. naughty acts
7. hit with the head
8. to wish for what someone else has

DOWN:

1. to be thankful for
2. thought about
3. hunger
4. sadness

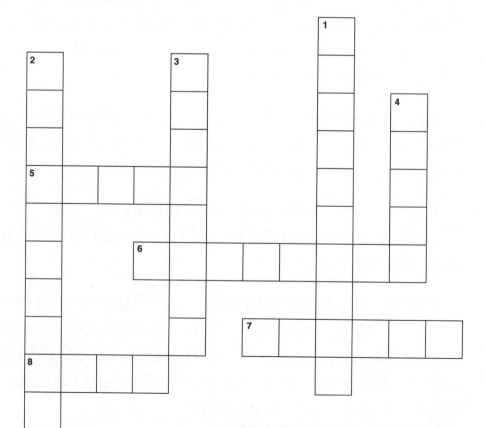

The Candlemaker

There once was a candlemaker from Brighton who made wonderful candles of all colors, shapes, and sizes. People came from near and far to admire and buy his candles. The candlemaker enjoyed making his candles so much that it did not seem right to ask people to pay for them. He gave candles away until there was none left to give.

One day, he reached into his cupboard for more dye, and there was none. He searched for more tallow, and there was none. He found string for the wick. However, without tallow or dye he could not make any candles. He had given away his last candle, and he did not know what to do.

He went to see his friend, the woodcutter.

"I have no candles to give to people," he said. "You will need to work very hard to chop wood today. People will depend on the light from their fireplaces." It was soon known throughout the country that there were no more beautiful candles to be bought in Brighton.

That evening, neighbors arrived with the woodcutter. They brought tallow and dye for the candlemaker. He was surprised and pleased. The candlemaker asked them why they had brought supplies.

"You have been giving us candles for years," answered the woodcutter. "Brighton would no longer be bright if you stopped making candles."

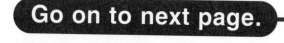

Go on to next page.

Directions

Answer each question about the story. Circle the letter in front of the correct answer.

1. Why does the candlemaker give away his candles?
   a. Candles are useful.
   b. Candles are beautiful.
   c. He enjoys making candles.
   d. Candles are easy to make.

2. Why does the candlemaker run out of tallow and dye?
   a. He forgets to buy more.
   b. He gives away his candles and has no money to buy more supplies.
   c. His supplies are late.
   d. He makes too many large candles.

3. The candlemaker _____.
   a. worries about the people who need candles
   b. finds more supplies
   c. tells people that there are no more candles
   d. asks the woodcutter to make candles

4. The neighbors _____.
   a. go to another city for candles
   b. buy wood from the woodcutter
   c. give tallow and dye to the candlemaker
   d. make their own candles

5. Why do the neighbors help the candlemaker?
   a. He asks for help.
   b. He helps them by giving them candles for light.
   c. The woodcutter asks for help.
   d. They run out of candles, too.

The Sand Castle

Many years ago, I spent my summers on the beach. Each year I built more fantastic sand castles. One special summer I built my most incredible sand castle. It had turrets and spires all over. Shells decorated its walls. There was a great moat around the castle and a drawbridge made of driftwood.

While I was admiring my effort, I heard a tiny voice. "Oh, it is magnificent! It is beautiful! I shall make my new home here in this lovely castle by the sea," said a small, sparkling fairy as she flew in and out of the windows.

Now, I had never seen a fairy, but I knew that I was seeing one then! "Little fairy," I said. "You can't live in a sand castle. It will only last until the sea comes and washes it away."

"But there has been a fire in my woods. I cannot find my people. I have no place to go. So I shall live in this castle until the sea washes us both away," she said sadly.

I had to think of a way to help the little fairy. "Come and live with me," I said. "You can stay near my window and come and go as you please. I promise you'll be safe."

We stayed at the beach until the sea came in and the castle slowly disappeared. Then the fairy agreed to come with me. She stayed with me all summer, then one morning very early there was a light tapping on my window. Her people had found my fairy! She was so happy; I tried not to be sad about her leaving. She said she would never forget me, and I know she has not. There have been times in the years since she left that I have felt sad. Then I would suddenly have a happy, warm feeling. And I would hear the little tinkle of fairy wings and know that there would always be a little magic in my life.

Go on to next page.

Name_____ Date_____

Directions

Read each sentence. Choose a word from the Word List that has the same meaning as the word or words in bold print. Write the word on the line.

Word List

incredible driftwood moat sand castles
fantastic drawbridge effort magnificent

1. The writer built **castles of sand** every summer._____

2. Every year they became more **amazing**. _____

3. One summer the writer built the most **unbelievable** sand castle. _____

_____

4. It had a great **ditch for water** all around it._____

5. There was a **bridge that goes up and down** made of wood. _____

_____

6. The writer used sand, shells, and **wood that had floated in on the**

water to make the castle special. _____

7. The writer heard the fairy while he was admiring his **work**._____

_____

8. The fairy thought it was **grand**. _____

Winter Wear

Once there was a kind woman named Mrs. McCan who lived all alone in a small cottage. The cottage had only a fireplace to heat it. Every winter Mrs. McCan bought wood for the fireplace and stayed nice and warm.

One winter there was no wood left to buy. Mrs. McCan did not know how she could stay warm. Mrs. McCan sat down to think about what she should do. While she thought, she began to knit a sweater. For many days Mrs. McCan sat and thought, knitting the entire time.

She stopped knitting one day and looked at the sweater. It was as big as the room.

"This is the answer!" Mrs. McCan said excitedly. She decided to knit a sweater for the cottage. Mrs. McCan measured the cottage and finished the sweater the next day.

To this day, every winter Mrs. McCan wraps a large, warm sweater around the cottage. She stays warm and cozy all winter.

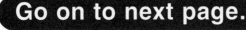

Go on to next page.

Directions

Answer each question about the story. Circle the letter in front of the correct answer.

1. Mrs. McCan first keeps her cottage warm with _____.
   a. a sweater
   b. a fire
   c. electric heat
   d. many clothes

2. Mrs. McCan cannot start a fire without _____.
   a. wood
   b. matches
   c. wet wood
   d. paper

3. What does Mrs. McCan do while thinking?
   a. She knits a sweater.
   b. She cooks dinner.
   c. She starts a fire.
   d. She chops wood.

4. How big is the sweater when Mrs. McCan first looks at it?
   a. It is as big as the woman.
   b. It is the size of the room.
   c. It is big enough to cover the cottage.
   d. It is larger than the cottage.

5. Mrs. McCan's idea to keep the cottage warm is to _____.
   a. find some wood
   b. move away
   c. knit a sweater for the cottage
   d. knit a blanket for the cottage

Clowning Around

Once there were two clowns who were the best of friends. They had been clowns together for several years at the same circus. They practiced their routines together. They showed each other their funniest faces. They helped each other to be better clowns. They were very happy— until one day.

In the circus was a grumpy man who never seemed to be happy unless he was making someone else unhappy. He couldn't stand happy people. He especially couldn't stand to watch those happy clowns getting along so well! So one day he hatched a nasty plan. He got each of the clowns alone. He told each clown that the other one thought he was the funnier clown.

At first, the friends didn't believe him. They knew he was a grumpy, unhappy man. Then they became suspicious of each other. They started to think the man was right. One night, they began their act as usual, but as it went on, they tried to outdo each other. They did more and more ridiculous things to make the people laugh. They were very funny. Then they began to knock each other over. At first, it was funny. Then they got rough. The children began to cry. The clowns were so involved with their competition that they didn't even notice.

Suddenly, the clowns heard loud, crazy laughter. It was the grumpy man! All at once, the clowns realized what they had done. They had frightened their favorite people, the children, by trying to be the best. All

they really wanted was to make the children laugh. When it was time for the clowns to perform again, they apologized to the crowd. Then they hugged and made up in such a silly way that all the children laughed again. Soon everyone was laughing—everyone but the grumpy old man!

Go on to next page.

Name_____   Date_____

Directions

Read each clue. Choose a word from the Word List that fits each clue. Write the words in the puzzle.

Word List
nasty   routines   apologized   competition
outdo   involved   ridiculous   suspicious

ACROSS:
4. actions done the same way every time
5. said that you were sorry
6. to do better
7. very silly
8. not nice

DOWN:
1. a struggle to be the best
2. not trusting
3. busy with

The Changing Man

There once was a man who could turn himself into any shape he wanted. Once he locked himself out of his house, and so he turned himself into a key and unlocked his door. Another time he turned into the shape of an airplane and flew around the world.

One day, a little girl ran up to him crying, "Oh, help me! My kitten is stuck in a drainpipe!"

The man told the girl he would rescue the kitten. The girl led him to the drainpipe. Then the man changed himself into the shape of a spring. He crawled into the pipe and told the girl to pull on his legs and then let go. She followed his directions exactly. The man sprang through the pipe, grabbed the kitten, and came out the other side.

The man quickly changed back to himself and gave the kitten to the girl. She thanked him and took her kitten home. Dusting himself off, the man continued walking down the street.

Go on to next page.

Directions

Answer each question about the story. Circle the letter in front of the correct answer.

1. Why does the man turn himself into a key?
   a. He likes the shape.
   b. His door is locked.
   c. It is the only shape he can make.
   d. A safe is locked.

2. The man can turn himself into _____.
   a. no shape
   b. one shape
   c. a few shapes
   d. any shape he wants

3. Why does the girl ask the man to help her?
   a. Her kitten is caught in a drainpipe.
   b. Her kitten is locked in an airplane.
   c. She loses her key.
   d. The girl cannot find her airplane.

4. The man asks the girl to _____.
   a. unlock the door
   b. fly an airplane
   c. pull on his legs
   d. crawl through the drainpipe

5. The man saves the kitten by _____.
   a. crawling through a pipe
   b. turning into a key
   c. jumping into an airplane
   d. springing through a drainpipe

Name _____   Date _____

Less Mess

Once upon a time, there was a little girl whose room was always very messy. Nothing her mother did could get the girl to keep her room clean. Occasionally, the mother would take the girl into her room and together they would pick up, put away, straighten, and clean all day. It would look so nice the mother would be sure that this time the girl would keep it that way. But the next day, it would be a disaster area once more.

The real reason that the girl did not clean her room was that she just didn't think there was any reason to do it. She didn't mind stepping over piles of clothes and toys to get to her bed. She didn't care if her games were all mixed together. She didn't even care on which end of the bed she put her head at night. So, why should she clean her room?

One day, however, all that changed. Her great-grandmother had given the little girl a very special ring. The old woman had told her it would bring her good fortune. The girl kept the ring on her finger all the time, and she did feel lucky. She was so excited!

But one morning she woke to find the ring was gone. It must have slipped from her finger! She tried frantically to look for the ring, but it was hopeless. She didn't know where to start.

So she did what she had to do. She began, piece by piece, to clean up her room. Finally, when every single item was in place, she found her ring. It was in a dainty glass dish on her bureau. She had never seen the dish before and she didn't know how the ring had gotten into it. But she did know that she was through with her messy ways! From then on, she kept her room neat as a pin, and she (almost) never lost anything!

Go on to next page.

Name _____   Date _____

Directions

Choose the word that best fits each sentence. Write the word in the blank.

1. The little girl's room was a _____.
   danger   disaster   present

2. Her mother could not get her to _____ her room.
   straighten   stretch   leave

3. The girl's great-grandmother told her the ring would bring good
   _____.
   feelings   food   fortune

4. She _____ looked for the ring.
   finally   frantically   never

5. It was _____ to look for the ring in her messy room.
   helpful   hopeful   hopeless

6. She put away every single _____.
   item   tool   idea

7. She found the ring on her _____.
   desk   bed   bureau

8. It was in a _____ glass dish.
   broken   dainty   dusty

Improving Reading Comprehension 3, SV 5801-9

A Gingerbread House

In a great forest, two children named Hansel and Gretel went for a walk. Suddenly, they came upon a beautiful house made of gingerbread and sweets.

"Look at this cottage, Gretel! Look at all the wonderful things to eat!" Hansel exclaimed.

"Let's go very quietly and taste the gingerbread!" Gretel said. So the two children went up to the house and tasted the gingerbread.

Inside the house, a mean woman waited for the children to come. When she heard them outside, she ran out and grabbed them and brought them into her house.

"What do you think you are doing? How dare you eat my house!" screamed the woman. "Just for that, you will stay here forever and rebuild my cottage."

The children began to rebuild the house. They mixed the batter for the gingerbread and asked the woman to check the oven to make sure it was hot enough.

"Hot enough! You children make sure that it is hot enough!" yelled the woman.

"But we do not know how," Hansel said.

"Yes, please show us," Gretel pleaded.

The woman decided it would be easier to show them, so she opened the oven door. As soon as she turned her back, the children quickly ran out of the house and down the road to their home.

Go on to next page.

Directions

Answer each question about the story. Circle the letter in front of the correct answer.

1. Why is the woman's house made of sweets?
   a. She likes to eat them.
   b. She wants children to come there.
   c. It is pretty.
   d. She wants birds to eat the sweets.

2. Why do the children eat the gingerbread?
   a. It looks delicious.
   b. Their mother makes it.
   c. They like to walk.
   d. They are sleepy.

3. What does the woman do to the children?
   a. plays with them
   b. chases them away
   c. makes them stay to rebuild her cottage
   d. cares for them

4. Why do Hansel and Gretel ask the woman to check the oven?
   a. to hide
   b. to keep warm
   c. so she will cook
   d. so they can run

5. How do Hansel and Gretel escape from the woman?
   a. They lock her in the house.
   b. They run away.
   c. The house falls on her.
   d. The gingerbread is good.

Lost and Found

Nancy and her father planned to hike up a mountain trail. The trail they chose was long and led to the top of a mountain. She and her father had packed a picnic lunch earlier in the morning. They both carried backpacks and a few other supplies.

As they started up the trail, Nancy's father pointed out many different flowers and trees. He showed Nancy the difference between the leaves of an oak tree and a maple tree. Soon, Nancy was pointing out different kinds of trees to her father.

"Look over there," Nancy whispered suddenly. They had just turned a corner of the trail. To the side of the path was a tiny baby raccoon. It appeared to be lost as it stumbled around in the tall grass.

"Its mother must be close by. Do you think we should stop here and watch it?" she asked.

"That's a good idea," her father answered. "We can eat our lunch while we watch the baby raccoon."

Nancy and her father sat beside the trail and ate their lunch. They watched the tiny raccoon until it tired itself out and fell asleep. Soon, a larger raccoon came through the bushes and sat down next to the baby raccoon.

Nancy and her father packed up their supplies and continued up the mountain. They knew the tiny raccoon was safe.

Go on to next page.

Directions

Answer each question about the story. Circle the letter in front of the correct answer.

1. Nancy and her father are going _____.
   a. to the top of a mountain
   b. to a park
   c. to eat lunch
   d. to look at trees

2. How does Nancy's father help her?
   a. He carries the supplies.
   b. He packs the picnic.
   c. He teaches her how to identify flowers and trees.
   d. He takes her to a park.

3. What kinds of trees do Nancy and her father see?
   a. cherry and birch
   b. apple and pine
   c. elm and birch
   d. oak and maple

4. What animal does Nancy see?
   a. a raccoon
   b. a squirrel
   c. a rabbit
   d. a fox

5. How do Nancy and her father help the animal?
   a. They find its mother.
   b. They feed it.
   c. They watch it so that nothing harms it.
   d. They take it home.

Dogs Deliver!

Have you ever seen a person walking along the street with a Seeing Eye dog? It seems amazing that these dogs know what to do. But they certainly do know what they're doing. They do it so well that the people they are with trust them completely. They trust the dogs with their lives!

Dogs do more for people than see. There are also dogs that help people hear. People who are deaf can have a dog that is trained to help them. These dogs are trained to hear certain types of noises, like telephones, doorbells, and their owner's name. When they hear these sounds, they go to their owners and lead them to the sound. When they hear a fire alarm, however, they do something quite different. They get their owner's attention and then lie down immediately. This tells the owner that it is time to get out quickly!

Dogs are also used to help children with spine injuries and other types of illness. These children, who are usually in wheelchairs, rely on their dogs for many things. The dogs are trained to open and close doors. They can ring doorbells. They can pick up things that the child drops—even coins! They can pull the wheelchair, and they can go and get help.

It is well known that animals can have a great positive influence on their owners. They make people feel calm and help them live healthier lives. Dogs are used in some hospital environments to help people get better. The dogs make people feel good. They are good friends. There is no doubt that the friendship developed between the working dog and its owner is one of the biggest benefits of all!

Go on to next page.

Directions ————————————————————

Rewrite each sentence. Use a word with the same meaning from the Word List in place of the underlined words.

Word List

rely   doubt   injuries   wheelchairs
influence   benefits   positive   environments

1. Many people <u>depend</u> on their working dogs for help. _____

    _____

2. Children with <u>damages</u> to their spines can use dogs. _____

    _____

3. These children are usually in <u>special chairs with wheels</u>. _____

    _____

4. Dogs are used in some hospital <u>surroundings; the things that are around you</u>.

    _____

5. The dogs have a <u>good</u> effect on the people's health. _____

    _____

6. The dogs can <u>have an effect on</u> the way people feel. _____

    _____

7. There is no <u>question</u> that friendships with dogs are good for most people.

    _____

8. The friendship between a dog and its owner is one of the best <u>helpful things</u> of all!

    _____

Name _____   Date _____

A New Name

Little Deer was tired of his name. It was a name for a young boy. Now that Little Deer was ten summers old, he no longer thought he was a little boy. Little Deer thought he was old enough to be given a powerful man's name. Little Deer knew he could not just change his name, so he talked to the elders of the tribe.

The elders of the tribe said Little Deer could earn a man's name by doing a brave deed. Little Deer could not think of a brave deed to do. Then one day Little Deer saw a wild horse charge toward his little sister. Without thinking of his own safety, Little Deer ran toward the horse, shouting and waving his arms. Just before the horse reached her, it turned away. The people of the tribe were so grateful to Little Deer that they changed his name to *Wild Horse*.

Go on to next page.

Directions

Answer each question about the story. Circle the letter in front of the correct answer.

1. Why is Little Deer unhappy?
   a. He does not like his name.
   b. He is not a young boy.
   c. The elders of the tribe do not listen to him.
   d. He is ten summers old.

2. What does Little Deer need to do to be given a new name?
   a. He needs to talk to the elders.
   b. He needs to do a brave deed.
   c. He needs to choose a new name.
   d. He needs to watch his sister.

3. Why does Little Deer run in front of a wild horse?
   a. He tries to catch it.
   b. He tries to save his sister.
   c. One of the elders tells him to do so.
   d. Little Deer wants to ride it.

4. What do the elders of the tribe do for Little Deer?
   a. They give him a party.
   b. They give him the wild horse.
   c. They name him *Wild Horse*.
   d. They ask him to watch all the children.

5. How will a new name change Little Deer's life?
   a. The tribe elders will come to him for advice.
   b. He will be responsible for the horses.
   c. The people of the tribe will no longer treat him like a child.
   d. He will be responsible for the children.

Going Batty!

What has fur and wings, flies at night, and sleeps upside down during the day? A bat, of course! Bats are the only flying mammals. They have fur, and their wings are made of leathery skin. The bones in their wings are made of an arm, extended fingers, and a thumb. Bats give birth to one or two young each year. The little bats huddle together in one place for warmth while the mother bats look for food.

Bats come in many sizes. The largest is the fruit bat. It can measure almost seven feet from wingtip to wingtip! Most bats eat insects or fruit. Some will eat small animals and fish. One bat can eat as many as 1,000 insects in an hour. Imagine how many insects we might have if there were no bats!

There are hundreds of different kinds of bats. They make up a huge portion of the mammals of the earth. Since bats are active at night, many people have never seen one. However, if you happen to live near a bridge that houses a bat colony, you may have seen a spectacular sight. During the warmer months, at dusk each day, the entire colony will take wing at once. They fly in swarms from their upside-down perches in search of insects. In some places, this sight is a regular attraction!

Go on to next page.

Directions

Choose the word that best fits each sentence. Write the word in the blank.

1. Bats are the only flying _____.
   animals   mammals   birds

2. The bones in a bat's wing are _____ fingers.
   extended   excellent   except

3. Young bats _____ together for warmth.
   hunger   fly   huddle

4. Bats make up a huge _____ of the mammal world.
   portion   pretend   picture

5. Sometimes a bat _____ will live under a bridge.
   cousin   colony   family

6. When all the bats fly at dusk, it is a _____ sight.
   speckled   spent   spectacular

7. The bats fly out in _____.
   singles   swarms   sweaters

8. Watching the bats swarm has become a regular _____
   in some places.
   attraction   action   problem

Oh, Deer!

Zach and Wendy went with their parents to the meadow for a picnic. After the picnic, Zach and Wendy wandered close to the forest to see the wildflowers growing there. Suddenly, a deer leaped out from behind a tree and stopped to look at them. When the deer ran back into the forest, Zach and Wendy followed it.

The deer ran straight down a well-worn path. It was not hard to follow the deer at first, but then the deer turned off the path and disappeared among the trees. Zach and Wendy could not see where the deer had gone, so they decided to return to the meadow.

Just then a bear stood up on the path close to them. Zach and Wendy stood very still, hoping the bear would go away. The bear did not move either. After a long minute, Zach grabbed Wendy's hand and started running down the path. They thought they heard the bear behind them, but when they turned around the bear was not there.

Zach and Wendy ran the rest of the way to the meadow. They shared their adventure with their parents. Both the children decided that deer looked best in a safe, open field.

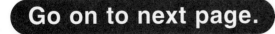
Go on to next page.

Directions

Answer each question about the story. Circle the letter in front of the correct answer.

1. What do Zach and Wendy do with their parents?
   a. They chase a deer into the forest.
   b. They look at wildflowers.
   c. They have a picnic in the meadow.
   d. They run away from a bear.

2. Why do Zach and Wendy go into the forest?
   a. to find more wildflowers
   b. to follow a deer
   c. to play a game
   d. to take a walk

3. What is in the path close to Zach and Wendy?
   a. a deer
   b. their parents
   c. bushes
   d. a bear

4. Why does the bear stand still?
   a. It is waiting to chase Zach and Wendy.
   b. It is hurt.
   c. It is afraid, too.
   d. It is looking for a friend.

5. What do Zach and Wendy decide when they go back to their parents?
   a. The forest is a good place to hide.
   b. It is not a good idea to chase a deer into the forest.
   c. The bear was not really chasing them.
   d. A picnic is not fun.

Don't Bug Me!

You may know that a spider is not an insect. Do you know why? What is an insect? What is the difference between an insect, like an ant, and a spider?

To be an insect, a creature must have five characteristics. First, it must breathe air. Second, its body must have three parts. The three parts are the head, the thorax, or the middle of the body, and the abdomen, which is at the back of the body. Third, an insect must have six legs. Fourth, an insect has a skeleton on the outside of its body. Fifth, an insect has no backbone.

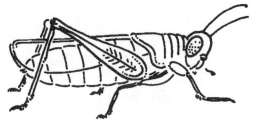

So how does the spider compare to an insect? Like an insect, a spider breathes air. A spider does not have a backbone. It also has a skeleton on the outside of its body. So far, the spider could be an insect. But here are the differences. A spider has two body parts, not three. And it has eight legs rather than six.

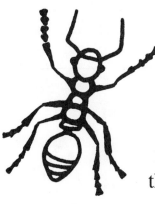

To some of us, all things creepy and crawly can go into one category. But the fact is, many of them, like the spider and the ant, are not the same!

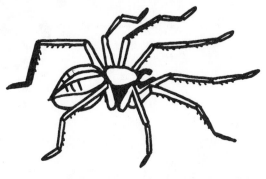

Go on to next page.

Name_____   Date_____

Directions

Choose the word from the Word List that best completes each sentence. Then use the remaining words from the Word List to label the three parts of the insect in the picture below.

Word List

category   insect   head   skeleton
thorax   compare   abdomen   characteristics

1. All insects have the same five _____.

2. This story was written to _____ spiders and insects.

3. Insects have a _____ on the outside of their body.

4. A spider is not an _____.

5. A spider is in a different _____ than an ant.

_____   _____

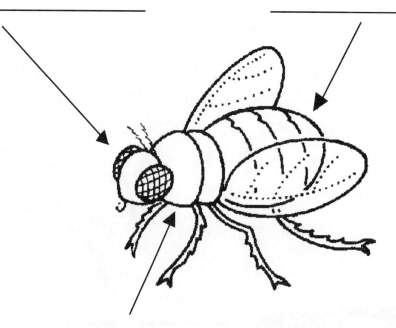

_____

Cat Facts

Cats are so common we see them almost every day. Millions of people have one or more cats as pets. They, along with dogs, are the most common pets we see. How much do we understand about our cats? We can tell when a cat is happy and when it is angry. But there are some things cats do that we may not fully understand.

Cats are descendants of wild cats. Many of the habits cats had in the wild are still the habits of our pets. Some of the things cats used to do in the wild are no longer necessary for cats that are pets. Cats still do them because they are instincts. Cats are born with these habits.

Many of these habits come from when cats are born. Kittens get milk from their mother. While they are drinking the milk, they push their paws in and out against the mother's stomach. This helps the milk come out. They also purr while they feed. This lets the mother know that everything is all right. When the cat becomes your pet, you become its "mother." You provide the food your cat eats. So when your cat jumps in your lap and presses its paws up and down on your legs and purrs, it is an action it remembers from being with its mother. Sometimes your cat will even drool while it does this. The cat's mouth is remembering the milk!

If you have a cat, you may want to gain more knowledge about it. There are many other interesting cat facts. You can locate them in your library.

Go on to next page.

Directions

Read each clue. Choose a word from the Word List that fits each clue. Write the words in the puzzle.

Word List

common   habits   provide

locate   instincts   millions   knowledge

ACROSS:

3. ways of behaving one is born with

5. a large number

6. give

7. find

DOWN:

1. what is known

2. things one is used to doing

4. everyday; not unusual

A Strange Adventure

When Madelaine traveled to Holland with her family, she had a strange adventure. The adventure was so strange that reporters interviewed her when she returned home. The story that Madelaine told them was something like this.

Madelaine had read many books about Holland and was curious about windmills. The first day in Holland, Madelaine took a walk so that she could see a windmill up close.

"I never knew windmills were so large," she said softly to herself.

"We have to be large. We have important work to do, and the wind is strong," responded the windmill.

Madelaine was so surprised she turned and ran into the nearest shop. The shop was full of wooden shoes.

"Who will believe that windmills can talk?" she asked herself.

"I'm not surprised," said a pair of wooden shoes. "Windmills are very powerful."

Madelaine raced from the store to find her parents. Before she could find them she had talked with a tulip, a bench, and a boat.

Go on to next page.

Directions

Answer each question about the story. Circle the letter in front of the correct answer.

1. Who went with Madelaine to Holland?
   a. her aunt
   b. her friends
   c. her family
   d. reporters

2. Why did reporters interview Madelaine?
   a. She had a strange adventure.
   b. She wrote a book.
   c. She asked them to.
   d. Her family asked them to.

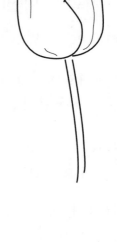

3. What spoke to Madelaine first?
   a. a tulip
   b. wooden shoes
   c. a windmill
   d. a boat

4. How did the talking windmill make Madelaine feel?
   a. silly
   b. afraid
   c. happy
   d. angry

5. Why would reporters want to write Madelaine's story?
   a. No one would believe it.
   b. No one would care about it.
   c. It would not be very interesting.
   d. Everyone would want to read it.

The Lighthouse

As Cameron guided his boat among the rocks, he looked up occasionally at the old lighthouse on the bluff. He had heard stories about the place. They said that it still lit up on stormy nights although it had been empty for years. Even the old lens was gone. There was no way a light could shine from the house now. Most people stayed away from the place anyway. They thought it was creepy.

Cameron forgot about the lighthouse for a while. Then one day while he was out on his boat, a sudden fog moved in around him. He couldn't see a thing. He used his radio to call his dad.

"Stay where you are, son," said his father. "This fog will lift soon enough and we'll get you out of there. I don't want you trying to move around those ledges now."

Cameron didn't like being fogged in. It made his skin crawl. He tried to relax. He was about to drop his anchor when he saw a light. It cut through the fog like a knife. Cameron couldn't believe his eyes. It was the lighthouse! For a moment, he wondered if it could be some kind of trick. What if the lighthouse had an evil spirit that would guide him right into the rocks? Cameron decided to trust the light. He started his engine and began to move slowly through the water.

Cameron made it home safely. His family didn't believe his story at first. But how else could he have gotten in past those rocks? Many people with more experience than Cameron had ended up wrecked in this kind of weather. Cameron knew just one thing for sure. He would never be afraid to go near the lighthouse again. Whatever was there had probably saved his life!

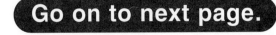

Go on to next page.

Directions

Rewrite each sentence. Use a word with the same meaning from the Word List in place of the underlined words.

Word List
bluff   experience   anchor   evil
wrecked   ledges   lens   occasionally

1. Cameron looked up at the old lighthouse <u>once in a while</u>. _____

_____

2. It stood on a <u>high piece of land</u>. _____

_____

3. The old lighthouse did not have a <u>glass to shine light</u> anymore. _____

_____

4. Cameron was afraid his boat would be <u>broken</u> on the rocks._____

_____

5. Many people with more <u>practice</u> had not made it. _____

_____

6. Cameron prepared to drop his <u>heavy weight</u> into the water. _____

_____

7. At first, Cameron thought the lighthouse might be <u>bad</u>. _____

_____

8. The lighthouse guided Cameron past the <u>sharp rocks</u>._____

_____

Message in a Bottle

Jeremy loved to walk by the sea. When he went to visit his cousin Michael on Cape Cod, they often spent hours walking along the beach. They would pretend they were pirates and look for shells and other treasures that the sea had left on the shore. Jeremy and Michael always made up stories as they walked.

Michael would call out to Jeremy, "Remember when we were lost at sea for two years?"

Jeremy would then add to the story, and they would take turns adding to the story all afternoon.

One day, as they were making up a story, Jeremy spotted a bottle next to a piece of driftwood.

"Look, Michael!" he cried as he picked up the bottle. "This is a real treasure!"

Jeremy quickly removed the cork, and a folded piece of paper dropped out. Michael held his breath as Jeremy carefully unfolded the note. On the note was a date, a name, an address, and the following message: "I am a young boy living in Canada. Please write to me and tell me about yourself and what you like to do."

Jeremy and Michael ran to Michael's house. They shared the note with Michael's family and wrote their new friend a letter.

Go on to next page.

Directions

Answer each question about the story. Circle the letter in front of the correct answer.

1. Where did Jeremy love to walk?
   a. through his neighborhood
   b. in the woods
   c. by the sea
   d. along the river

2. What did Jeremy and Michael do as they walked?
   a. tricks
   b. made up stories
   c. told jokes
   d. their homework

3. What did they find next to the driftwood?
   a. a small animal
   b. a pirate treasure
   c. an old doll
   d. a bottle

4. Why did the boy from Canada write the note?
   a. He hated to write.
   b. He wanted to run away.
   c. He wanted a pen pal.
   d. He needed help.

5. How did Jeremy and Michael feel about the note?
   a. They were excited.
   b. They thought it was funny.
   c. They didn't care about it.
   d. They thought the boy was silly.

Night Fright

Carlos was camping with his friend Andrew and his family. Carlos and Andrew had a tent to themselves. They had had a long, busy day hiking and canoeing, and now they were ready to sleep. They snuggled deep into their sleeping bags, closed their eyes, and fell asleep immediately.

Suddenly, Carlos was wide awake. He sat up and discovered that Andrew was also awake. Carlos' heart was beating fast.

"Did you hear that noise?" asked Andrew. "Something is moving around outside the tent!"

"What is it?" asked Carlos. "It sounds really big! Get your flashlight and shine it out the door!"

Andrew carefully unzipped the tent. He shined his light out into the dark night. The night was very black and the boys couldn't see a thing. It was also very quiet. Then they heard it again—something was circling their tent! The boys froze in fear and their hair stood on end.

Then they heard, "Hey! What are you guys doing awake?" The boys both yelled. Andrew dropped his flashlight and Carlos fell out of the tent. "Whoa! It's just me, boys," said Andrew's father. "I was just checking around the area making sure everything was secure."

"Good grief, Dad! You just about scared us to death!" Andrew exclaimed.

"So I see!" said his father, laughing. "Go on back to sleep now. I don't think you'll hear any more noises tonight."

Go on to next page.

Name_____ Date_____

Directions

Read each clue. Choose a word from the Word List that fits each clue. Write the words in the puzzle.

Word List

exclaimed   immediately   canoeing   area
hiking   secure   circling   discovered

ACROSS:
3. right away
4. a type of boating
7. going around
8. a certain space

DOWN:
1. a type of walking
2. found
5. safe
6. spoke with feeling

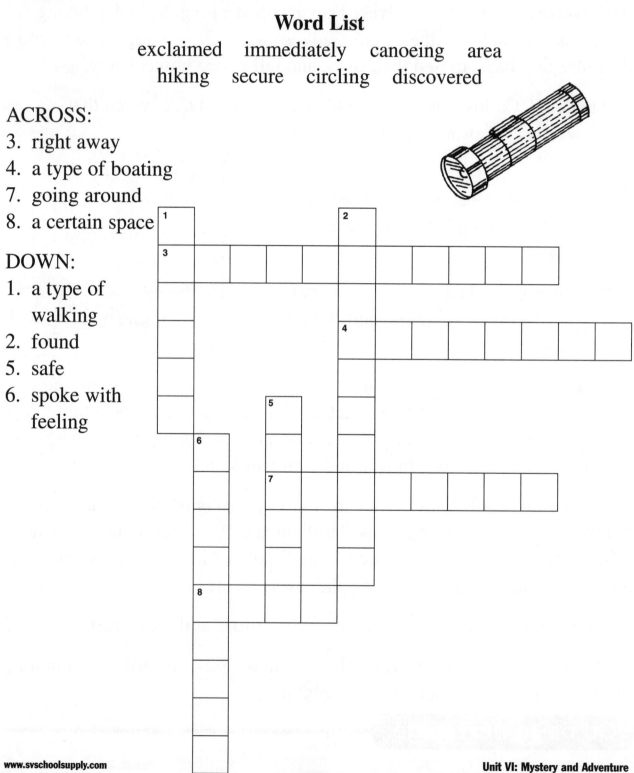

Wilbur Fapes

"I am an artist,"
Said Wilbur Fapes.
"I don't paint pictures;
I design escapes.

"If you're trapped in a well,
Or caught in a tree,
Just give me a call—
I can set you free.

"If your sister locks a door,
And can't find the key,
like magic in a minute,
I can set her free.

"If your kite is trapped
In a tall, tall tree,
Don't leave it there—
I can set it free.

"If you're tired of the jungle,
And want to escape,
Don't try to find your way alone,
Ask for Wilbur Fapes."

Go on to next page.

Directions

Answer each question about the story. Circle the letter in front of the correct answer.

1. What kind of an artist is Wilbur Fapes?
   a. one who paints
   b. one who draws
   c. one who escapes
   d. one who shapes clay

2. How can Wilbur help if you are locked in?
   a. He can set you free.
   b. He can join you.
   c. He can give you some food.
   d. He can talk to you.

3. If your kite is in a tree, what can Wilbur do?
   a. pull it out
   b. get you a new kite
   c. set the kite free
   d. cut down the tree

4. What kind of writing tells Wilbur's story?
   a. a story
   b. a poem
   c. cartoon
   d. a song

5. How does Wilbur probably feel about his talent?
   a. disappointed
   b. angry
   c. embarrassed
   d. proud

Monster Mystery

What if a huge serpent were living in a deep lake? What if it had been there for many years? What if many people had seen this creature, even taken pictures of it, yet no one really knew for sure if it actually existed?

Well, that is the case with one of the mysteries of the world today. The lake is Loch Ness in Scotland. The so-called monster is the Loch Ness Monster. It has been given the nickname "Nessie." Many years ago, a man claimed to have seen the monster. It had a little head, a long neck, and a huge body and tail. Since then, other people visiting the lake have said that they, too, have seen Nessie. They all describe a similar creature. Some people have taken pictures of what they saw. But there is no way to know if the pictures are real. Scientists have spent weeks on the lake with special equipment. They sent out sonar, or sound waves, that would hit against anything in the water. The waves would come back to the boat. This would show the scientists where the monster was. The scientists tried to find Nessie. But the lake is very deep and dark. There was no sign of any monster.

People still say they have seen this strange monster of the lake. Some people believe that Nessie really does exist. Others believe that people only think they see a monster. They think the pictures are fake. We may never know if Nessie is really there. The Loch Ness may keep its secrets forever!

Go on to next page.

Name _____   Date _____

Directions

Read each sentence. Choose a word from the Word List that has the same meaning as the word or words in bold print. Write the word on the line.

Word List

actually   sonar   claimed   serpent
creature   existed   similar   nickname

1. This story is about a **living being** in a lake. _____

2. People have given the monster the **pet name** "Nessie." _____

3. Some people think it has **been there** for many years. _____

4. Nessie has been described as a huge **snake-like animal**. _____

5. Most people have **alike** descriptions of the monster. _____

6. Over the years, many people have **said that it was true** that they

   have seen Nessie. _____

7. Scientists went to the lake with **sound**

   wave equipment. _____

8. There is no way to know if Nessie is **in fact** in

   the lake. _____

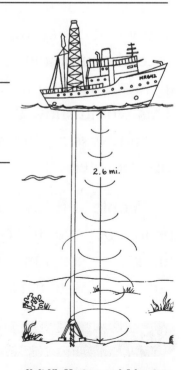

2.6 mi.

Soapy Business

Kiley Riley hurried home from school to check the mail. On the kitchen table there was a box that was addressed to her. She ran to her room and opened the box. It contained a bar of *Secret Soap*.

The directions said, "Wash evenly to completely disappear. Use again to reappear."

"I need to test this soap," Kiley said. "If I wash my feet and they disappear, I can put on my socks and shoes. Then no one will notice that my feet are gone."

The next morning Kiley washed her feet with the soap, and they disappeared! She ran to the kitchen.

"Mother, my feet have disappeared!" she cried.

"They are under your knees. Good morning, and eat your breakfast," her mother replied.

When Kiley went to school, she quickly forgot that her feet were invisible. It was like a normal day.

The following morning Kiley planned to have an exciting day. She made herself and her clothes completely invisible. When Kiley walked through the kitchen, her mother did not see her. Eric Clark did not see her and almost rode over her with his bicycle. The crossing guard did not see her, and Kiley was almost hit by a car. The teacher did not see her and closed the door in Kiley's face. Kiley decided that this was not a good idea. She carefully walked home and used the soap to become visible again.

Go on to next page.

Directions

Answer each question about the story. Circle the letter in front of the correct answer.

1. What does Kiley find on the kitchen table?
   a. mail
   b. a box addressed to her
   c. a notebook
   d. a postcard

2. What is in the box?
   a. a book
   b. a gift
   c. a bar of soap
   d. a pair of socks

3. What does *Secret Soap* do?
   a. It makes beautiful bubbles.
   b. It makes Kiley disappear.
   c. It cleans.
   d. It does not do anything.

4. At school, why does Kiley forget that her feet are invisible?
   a. Her feet are there.
   b. Her best friends do not notice that her feet are invisible.
   c. She is wearing socks and shoes.
   d. Her feet are not invisible.

5. By the end of the school day, Kiley might think that being invisible
   is _____.
   a. dangerous
   b. fun
   c. silly
   d. exciting

Improving Reading Comprehension
Grade 3

Answer Key

P. 7
1. silent
2. diamonds
3. peaceful
4. snowball
5. through

P. 8
1. gather
2. filtering
3. avoided
4. pecked
5. remaining

P. 9
1. b
2. c
3. a

P. 10
ACROSS
1. swarms
4. mammals
5. portion
DOWN
2. attraction
3. colony

P. 12
Sentences using the following words:
1. informed
2. project
3. scarcely
4. prepared
5. endless
6. bursting
7. bruising
8. prevent

P. 14
1. a
2. b
3. d
4. b
5. b

P. 16
1. c
2. a
3. c
4. a
5. c

P. 18
1. classmates
2. curiously
3. season
4. describe
5. forms
6. sleet
7. eagerly
8. suggestions

P. 20
1. d
2. a
3. b
4. c
5. a

P. 22
ACROSS
4. temperature
6. seasons
7. brilliant
8. habits
DOWN
1. extreme
2. humid
3. equator
5. lengths

P. 24
1. b
2. d
3. c
4. a
5. d

P. 26
1. b
2. a
3. d
4. a
5. b

P. 28
1. talented
2. graceful
3. ballerina
4. Artists
5. patterns
6. unaware
7. simple
8. tangled

P. 30
1. c
2. a
3. d
4. b
5. d

P. 32
Sentences using the following words:
1. longingly
2. pleasant
3. reflecting
4. urge
5. opportunity
6. appetite
7. precious
8. freedom

P. 34
1. c
2. b
3. a
4. b
5. d

P. 36
1. scowling
2. grumbled
3. boring
4. fault
5. starved
6. poisonous
7. skittering
8. absolutely

P. 38
ACROSS
3. female
7. separated
8. protect
DOWN
1. male
2. solved
4. advertise
5. shelter
6. hutch

P. 40
1. b
2. b
3. c
4. d
5. a

P. 42
1. prepared
2. necessary
3. discussed
4. expensive
5. success
6. volunteered
7. aquarium
8. event

P. 44
Sentences using the following words:
1. nursery
2. haunted
3. concerned
4. explanation
5. nervous
6. annoying
7. ruin
8. investigation

P. 46
1. c
2. b
3. d
4. b
5. c

P. 48
1. gather
2. filtering
3. comforting
4. remaining
5. ovals
6. favored
7. treatment
8. fetch

P. 50
1. unusual
2. investigate
3. amusing
4. complained
5. fierce
6. due
7. occasionally
8. sorted

P. 52
ACROSS
5. stole
6. mischief
7. butted
8. envy
DOWN
1. appreciate
9. considered
10. appetite
11. grief

P. 54
1. c
2. b
3. a
4. c
5. b

P. 56
1. sand castles
2. fantastic
(or incredible)
3. incredible
(or fantastic)
4. moat
5. drawbridge
6. driftwood
7. effort
8. magnificent

P. 58
1. b
2. a
3. a
4. b
5. c

P. 60
ACROSS
4. routines
5. apologized
6. outdo
7. ridiculous
8. nasty
DOWN
1. competition
2. suspicious
3. involved

P. 62
1. b
2. d
3. a
4. c
5. d

P. 64
1. disaster
2. straighten
3. fortune
4. frantically
5. hopeless
6. item
7. bureau
8. dainty

P. 66
1. b
2. a
3. c
4. d
5. b

P. 68
1. a
2. c
3. d
4. a
5. c

P. 70
Sentences using the
following words:
1. rely
2. injuries
3. wheelchairs
4. environments
5. positive
6. influence
7. doubt
8. benefits

P. 72
1. a
2. b
3. b
4. c
5. c

P. 74
1. mammals
2. extended
3. huddle
4. portion
5. colony
6. spectacular
7. swarms
8. attraction

P. 76
1. c
2. b
3. d
4. c
5. b

P. 78
1. characteristics
2. compare
3. skeleton
4. insect
5. category
Label head,
abdomen, and thorax.

P. 80
ACROSS
3. instincts
5. millions
6. provide
7. locate
DOWN
1. knowledge
2. habits
4. common

P. 82
1. c
2. a
3. c
4. b
5. d

P. 84
Sentences using the
following words:
1. occasionally
2. bluff
3. lens
4. wrecked
5. experience
6. anchor
7. evil
8. ledges

P. 86
1. c
2. b
3. d
4. c
5. a

P. 88
ACROSS
3. immediately
4. canoeing
7. circling
8. area
DOWN
1. hiking
2. discovered
5. secure
6. exclaimed

P. 90
1. c
2. a
3. c
4. b
5. d

P. 92
1. creature
2. nickname
3. existed
4. serpent
5. similar
6. claimed
7. sonar
8. actually

P. 94
1. b
2. c
3. b
4. c
5. a